PRAYERS FOR LITTLE PEOPLE

WRITTEN BY
SARAH FLETCHER

ART BY
DON KUEKER

1476

Publishing House
St. Louis   London

Ask, and it will be given you;
seek, and you will find;
knock, and it will be opened to you.

Matthew 7:7 RSV

IN THE MORNING

I wake up to another day,
Another day to learn and play.
There's one thing I just have to say:
THANK YOU, GOD!

The world is beautiful, it's true,
And every day brings something new
To show the love that comes from You.
THANK YOU, GOD!

A CHRISTMAS PRAYER

Long ago in Bethlehem
A little King was born.
Dear God, You sent Your Son to earth
That frosty Christmas morn.

You sent Him here to save the world
From sin and death and pain.
Dear God, I ask that in my heart
Your King will ever reign.

A GIFT FOR JESUS

Jesus, when the wise men came
They brought You gifts of gold
And frankincense and myrrh—
It was a splendid sight, I'm told.

I'm just a little child, and yet,
I want to do my part.
And so, dear Jesus, for my gift
I bring to You my heart.

FOR MY FRIENDS

Jesus, bless my little friends.
Bless my big friends too.
Help us all to live and love
And grow to be like You.

FOR GROWN-UPS

Thank You, Lord, for those who love me,
Care for me, and teach of You.
Lead me in the paths of Your love.
Bless them, Lord, and lead them too.

AS I GROW

Jesus grew to be a man
So long ago in Galilee.
Went to show His Father's love,
Went to set His people free.

I'll grow up as Jesus did,
But even while I'm very small,
Help me, God, to be like Him,
To show Your love to one and all.

HELPING

Help me, Jesus, every day
To show Your love in my own way,
In all my work, in all my play,
In what I do and what I say.

WHEN I HURT

Jesus, when I'm hurt or ill,
Help me know You're with me still.
Fix whatever might be wrong.
Make me better, make me strong.

FOR ALL CHILDREN

Friend of children long ago,
You're my Friend; You've told me so.
Please bless all children everywhere
And keep them in Your loving care.

WHEN I'M AFRAID

Jesus, I'm a little frightened.
I don't know just what to do.
Help me know You're always with me.
Help me, Lord, to trust in You.

MY SONG

Jesus, You are my Friend,
My Helper kind and true.
Therefore I will praise You
In everything I do.

ABOUT PRAYING

Jesus, teach me how to pray
With all my heart, in every way.
Anytime and anywhere
I know You'll always hear my prayer.

FOR FORGIVENESS

On the cross of Calvary,
Dearest Lord, You died for me.
Help me, Lord; my sins forgive.
Teach me, Lord, like You to live.

AN EASTER PRAYER

Jesus Christ, my risen King,
Hear the prayer of thanks I bring.
Thanks for breaking death's dark door,
Thanks for life forevermore.

WITH JESUS ALWAYS

Jesus, let me walk with You,
Although my steps are small.
Stay beside me, hold my hand,
And never let me fall.

A TABLE PRAYER

Thank You for the food we eat.
Let children everywhere
Have just as much to thank You for.
Please, God, hear our prayer.